Mary Jones
& Her Bible

This book is dedicated to my wife Liz, also a Jones from Wales.

Mary Jones
& Her Bible

The Original Story
by
Mary Ropes (M.E.R.)

Presented Here in a New Version
Edited and Revised by
Chris Wright

Sonlight
Curriculum Ltd.

Text and Illustrations
Copyright © 2007 Chris Wright
Cover Design and Illustration
by Dave Lilly

English Scriptures and additional materials quoted are from the *Good News Bible* © 1994 published by the Bible Societies/HarperCollins Publishers Ltd., *UK Good News Bible* © American Bible Society 1966, 1971, 1976, 1992. Used with permission.

Welsh Scriptures quoted are from the Welsh Bible published in Rhydychen (Oxford) in 1799, and bought by Mary Jones in 1800.

ISBN 978-1-887840-85-9

Sonlight Curriculum, Ltd.
8042 S. Grant Way
Littleton, CO 80122
www.sonlight.com

MARY JONES AND HER BIBLE

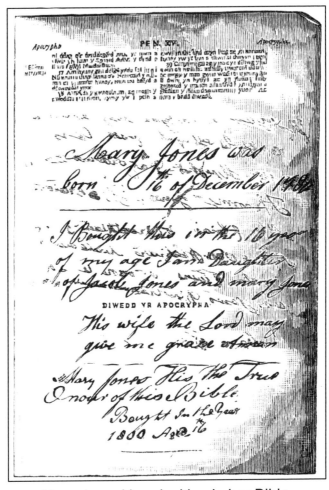

Mary Jones' handwriting in her Bible

Mary Jones was born 16th of December 1784.
I bought this in the 16th year of my age. I am Daughter of
Jacob Jones and Mary Jones His wife.
the Lord may give me grace. Amen
Mary Jones His the True Onour [is the true owner] of this
Bible. Bought in the Year 1800 Aged 16th

INTRODUCTION

This is a true story, showing how much God needs ordinary people. As the story unfolds, you will see how a girl here, a preacher there, a schoolmaster who couldn't read or write, were slowly being drawn together to be part of something that just couldn't be stopped.

All over the world today people are busy translating the Bible into different languages. Others are busy distributing copies. The Bible Societies print and distribute millions of Bibles around the world, in over 2,000 languages. Every year there are almost 400,000,000 copies of parts of the Bible distributed, and over 26,000,000 complete Bibles. Many of these are given away or sold at a nominal price. You can find the full story on the www.biblesociety.org website.

The English verses used in this book have been taken from the Good News Bible (also known as Today's English Version), published by the Bible Societies. The Welsh verses are from Mary Jones' Bible, and are the exact words that she read and learnt.

We're calling her Mary in this book, but her name is Mari Jones in Welsh. You can see the remains of Mary's cottage, Ty'n-y-Ddôl, if you go to Llanfihangel-y-Pennant in mid-Wales. Go past the church of Saint Michael and keep on until you come to a small bridge over the river. The public road comes to an end just here.

Although the cottage is in ruins, the lower part of the walls has been preserved and a stone monument has been built inside. The most interesting thing to me is the large old fireplace, which would surely be able to tell a few tales of Mary Jones if it could talk. The river runs at the back of Ty'n-y-Ddôl – the name means The House in the Meadow – just as it did when Mary Jones lived there. The whole area is so unchanged that you will see many things just as Mary saw them.

Step now into this book, and travel back over 200 years in time. Although the people would be speaking in Welsh, we will have to 'listen' in English.

This story is based on a famous book written by Mary Ropes (M.E.R.) in 1882, and reprinted many, many times. The illustrations used here come from early copies of her book. In the original book, Mary Ropes uses the character of Mary's father to help tell the early part of the story. You might think that a book published not long after Mary died would be very accurate, and in general it is, but recent research has discovered that Mary's father Jacob died when she was aged four. I have therefore not included Mary's father in this story.

Mary Ropes may have got some of her account from Lizzie Rowlands, a young woman who knew Mary Jones well in her old age, right up to the time of Mary's death in 1864. However, Mary Jones was nearly eighty when she talked with Lizzie Rowlands, and she may have been forgetful on some things, as she never kept a journal.

Lizzie Rowlands does not seem to have written down what she was told until much later. This helps explain why over the years slightly differing accounts of Mary Jones' life have appeared, and it's hard to be sure about some details. However, these differences are unimportant in the overall story. This is the version told by Mary Ropes, with some corrections and a few additions that are the result of modern research.

A mistake by nearly everyone, until recently, is the belief that Mary was sixteen when she walked to Bala in the spring or early summer of 1800. Even the monument placed in the remains of Mary's cottage in the early 1900s says she was sixteen. We now know that Mary was born just before Christmas in 1784. This of course makes her fifteen in the early summer of 1800, so her achievement is even more amazing. Mary's baptismal certificate exists today, and if you look carefully at Mary's handwriting in her Bible, you can see that she says: "I bought this in the 16th year of my age," and again: "Bought in the year 1800 aged 16th," which of course means she was fifteen.

Remember, not only was Mary Jones a real person, but the story is still going on today. Will *you* be part of it?

Chris Wright

Welsh is a very difficult language for English speaking people to pronounce. Here is a very quick guide to some of its letters.

'c' sounds like a k, as in KIT.

'ch' sounds like ch in LOCH (a 'wet' sounding K).

'dd' sounds like th, as in THERE.

'f sounds like a v, as in VERY.

'ff sounds like an f, as in FAR.

'g' is hard-sounding, as in GET.

'll' sounds like a mixture of th and l (a hard one, this), with a bit of throat-clearing mixed in.

'u' sounds like ee, as in BEEN, but 'au' is pronounced like i, as in NINE, in many areas.

'w' is more like oo, as in SOON, than the English w sound.

'y' is like a u, as in UNDER, except in the last syllable when it sounds like i, as in SIT.

There are some exceptions to these pronunciations, but I did warn you that the language is difficult. Try saying Llanfihangel.

CHAPTER 1

At the Foot of the Mountains

Mary Jones pulled her shawl tightly around her shoulders, and darted across the lane. There was no one to see her as she ran.

The night shadows had fallen around the little Welsh village of Llanfihangel-y-Pennant. It was late autumn in 1792, and a cold wind moaned and sighed among the trees, stripping them of their leaves – now no longer bright green – whirling them round, and laying them in shivering heaps along the narrow lane.

The few stone cottages in the valley seemed to be hiding below the mountain of Cadair Idris, with its dark crags and rocky precipices. Far away in the distance lay Cardigan Bay, with white breakers rolling in to dash into foam. The pale moon lit up peaked masses of cloud that looked like another ghostly Cadair Idris in the sky.

Mary Jones looked back over her shoulder. A warm light shone through the window of one of the cottages.

The light came from the blaze of a fire of dried driftwood in the stone hearth, and also from a rush light, throwing its somewhat uncertain brightness upon a weaver's loom. A bench, two or three stools, a cupboard, and a kitchen table – these, with the loom, were the only pieces of furniture. The cottage was Mary's home, where she lived with her mother.

A Welsh cottage from Mary Ropes' book, but much larger than the one in which Mary Jones was brought up. Turn to the end of the book to see what Mary's cottage probably looked like.

Standing in the center of the room was a woman dressed in a cloak and a black hat. "It's not like you to be late for the meeting, Mary," she said, when Mary hurried back inside. "It must be gone six o'clock. You've been a long time getting that lantern."

Mary raised a pair of bright eyes to her mother's face. "Yes, mother," she replied, "I was so long because I ran to borrow neighbor Williams' lantern. The latch of ours won't hold, and there's such a wind tonight that I knew we should have the light blown out."

"There's a moon," Mrs. Jones said, "and I could have done without a lantern."

"Yes, but then I should have had to stay at home," Mary replied, for she knew that it would not be safe for her to go without a light. Then she added, "And I do so love to go."

"You needn't tell me that, child," Molly laughed. "I don't think there's anyone as willing as you. You already know all I can teach you of the Bible, as I learnt it."

The cottage was called Ty'n-y-Ddôl. Mary opened the door, and she and her mother sallied out into the cold windy night.

The moon had disappeared now behind the thick dark cloud, and Mary's borrowed lantern was very useful. Carefully she held it, so that the light fell upon the way they had to go, a way that would have been difficult if not dangerous without its friendly aid. "Llusern *yw* dy air i'm traed, a llewyrch i'm llwybr," Mrs. Jones said quietly, remembering the words from Psalm 119 in the Welsh Bible as she took her daughter's hand. "Your word is a lamp to guide me and a light for my path."

"Yes, mother, that's what I was just thinking," Mary replied, holding on tightly. "I wish I knew more verses like that."

Mrs. Jones sighed. "How glad I should be if I could teach you more. But it is many years since I learned, and we have no Bible, and my memory is not as good and it used to be."

A walk of some length along a rough road brought them at last to the little meeting-house at the farm in Llechwedd, where the members belonging to the Methodists were gathered.

Mary and her mother were rather late, and the mid-week service had begun, but farmer Evans made room for them on his bench.

Mary was the only child there, but she was so willing to listen and to learn that no one looking at her could have felt that she was out of place. Indeed, the members who met there had come to look upon Mary as one of their number, and made her very welcome.

When the meeting was over, Mary relit the lantern and was ready to accompany her mother home. But Farmer Evans put his great broad hand on Mary's shoulder, saying, "Well, my little maid, you're rather young for these meetings, though the Lord has need of lambs as well as sheep. And He is well pleased when the lambs learn to hear His voice early, even in their tender years."

Then with a gentle smile the old man released the girl, and turned away. He knew that in Mary's face there was a promise of power for good.

"Why *don't* we a Bible of our own, mother?" Mary asked as she trotted homeward, lantern in hand.

"Because Bibles are scarce, child, and we're too poor to pay the price for one. A weaver's is an honest trade, but we don't get rich by it. With your father now dead, we must think ourselves happy if we can keep the wolf from the door, and have clothes to cover us. Still, precious as the Word of God would be in our hands, it is more important that its teachings and its truths find a place in our hearts. I tell you, my girl, they who come to know the love of God, have discovered the greatest truth that the Bible can teach them. And those who are trusting Jesus for their pardon and peace, and for eternal life, can wait patiently to find out more of His word and will."

"I suppose *you* can wait, mother, because you've waited so long that you're used to it," Mary replied. "But it's harder for me. Every time I hear something read out of the Bible, I long to hear more. But if I could *read*, it would be harder still not to have a Bible of our own."

Mrs. Jones was about to answer, when she stumbled over a large stone and fell, though fortunately without hurting herself. Mary's thoughts were so full of what she had been saying, that she had become careless in holding the lantern high.

"Ah, child, it's the present duties that we must look after most," Molly said, as she got slowly up. "And even a fall may teach us a lesson. The very Word of God itself, which is a lamp to our feet and a light to our path, can't save us from many a tumble if we don't use it the right way. If we let the light shine on our daily life, the Lord will help us in all that we do. Remember this, Mary."

And Mary did remember, and her life proved that she had taken the lesson to heart – a simple lesson taught by her mother who loved the Lord, and a lesson that she treasured up in her very heart of hearts. The Word of God – the Bible – the most important book in the world, and a light for the way.

Cadair Idris

CHAPTER 2

Mrs. Evans' Promise

In the homes of poor people, where the older members of
the family were needed to earn enough money for food
and clothing, the children learnt to be useful very early.
Girls of six or seven could take charge of a younger
brother and sister, while many other children of that age
ran errands, did the shopping, and made themselves of
very real use for much of the day.

Such was the case in Mary's family. Jacob and Molly
had been weavers of woolen cloth, so much of which used
to be made in Wales. Mary's father died when she was
only four, so many of the household duties became her
responsibility. At an age when children of richer parents
were amusing themselves with their toys or books, Mary
was sweeping, and dusting, and scrubbing, and digging,
and weeding to help her mother.

It was Mary who fed the few hens and looked for their
eggs, so often laid in out-of-the-way places, rather than in
the nest.

 It was Mary who took care of the hive, and who never feared the bees; and it was Mary again who, when more active duties were done, would draw a low stool towards the hearth in winter or outside the cottage door in summer, and try to make or mend her own clothes. Often she would be singing to herself in Welsh a verse or two of a hymn she had learnt in chapel, or repeating texts that she had picked up and retained in her quick and eager mind.

In the long light summer evenings she chose to sit where she could see the majestic form of the mountain of Cadair Idris, with its varying lights and shadows as the sun sank lower and lower in the horizon. And in her imagination this mountain was made to play many a part, as she recalled the stories that her mother had told her, and the chapters she had heard read at chapel.

So Cadair Idris became the mountain in the land of Moriah where Abraham was sent with Isaac. Then Mary would fix her great dark eyes upon the rocky steeps before her, until she fancied she could see Abraham and his son toiling up towards the place of sacrifice, the boy bearing the wood for the burnt offering.

More and more vividly the whole scene would grow upon her fancy, until the picture seemed to be almost a reality, and she could imagine that she heard Abraham's voice borne faintly to her ear by the breeze that fanned her cheek – a voice that replied almost sadly to his son's question about the offering, in the words, "Duw a edrych iddo ei hun am oen y poeth-offrwm – God Himself will provide one." Genesis 22:8.

Then the scene would change. Night was drawing near and Cadair Idris, taking on softer outlines, became the mountain where Jesus went to pray.

Leaving the large crowd who had been trying to hear His every word – leaving even His disciples whom He loved – there was Jesus, alone save for His Father's presence, praying, and refreshing His weary spirit after the work and trials and sorrows of the day.

"If I'd only lived in those days," Mary sighed sometimes. "How I should have loved Him. *And* He'd have taught me, perhaps, as He did those two who walked such a long way with Him on the road to Emmaus, without knowing it was Jesus; only I think *I* should have known Him, just through love."

Nor was it only the mountain of Cadair Idris with which Mary associated scenes from Bible history. The Dysynni Valley, in the upper end of which Llanfihangel-y-Pennant was situated, ran down to the sea by a place called Tywyn. And whenever she happened to be near, Mary would sit on the shore and gaze across the blue-green waters of Cardigan Bay, and dream of the Sea of Galilee, and of Jesus who walked upon its waters. She thought of Jesus as He stilled the raging storm with a word. She thought of Him as He sometimes chose to make a boat His pulpit, and preach to the people standing upon the shore. She saw them clustered to the very edge of the water, so that they might not lose a word of the precious things that He spoke.

One afternoon Mary's mother was seated at her loom, and Mary was sewing a patch into an almost worn-out dress of her own. Suddenly a tap at the door of Ty'n-y-Ddôl was followed by the entrance of Mrs. Evans the farmer's wife, a kind motherly woman who was looked up to and loved by many of the Llanfihangel villagers.

"Good day to you, Molly," she said cheerily, her face all aglow. "And my Mary, too – I used to come here when you were small and running round on your sturdy pins as fast as many a bigger child. Don't I remember you then, You'd keep a deal stiller than any mouse if your father would tell a story you could understand, more particular if it was out of the Bible. Daniel and the Lions, or David and the Giant, or Peter in the Prison – these were the favorites then. Yes, and the history of Joseph and his brothers. Only you used to cry when you heard how his brothers put Joseph in the pit, and went home and told Jacob that wicked lie that almost broke the old man's heart."

"She's as fond of anything of that sort now as she was then," said Molly Jones, pausing in her work; "or rather she's fonder than ever. With her father dead, I only wish I was able to give Mary a bit of schooling. It seems hard, for she is willing enough, and it's high time she was learning something. Why, Mrs. Evans, she can't read yet, because there's no one here to teach her."

Mary looked up, her eyes opening wide. "Oh, if I only *could* learn," she cried eagerly. "It's so horrible not to know how to read. If I could, I would read all those stories myself, and not trouble *anyone* to tell them."

"You forget, Mary, we have no Bible," her mother said, "and we cannot afford to buy one either, so dear and scarce they are."

"Yes," Mrs. Evans replied, "it's a great need in our country of Wales. My husband was telling me only the other day that this shortage of Welsh Bibles is getting to be spoken of everywhere. Even those who can afford to pay for them find there are none available, as often as not. And poor people can't get them at all. But we hope a Society in London may print some more soon. It won't be before they're wanted, either.

"But with all this talk, Mrs. Jones," continued the farmer's wife, "I'm forgetting my errand in coming here, and that was to ask if you have any new-laid eggs. I've a large order sent me, and our hens are laying badly, so that I can't make up the number. I've been collecting a few here and there, but I haven't enough yet."

"Mary knows more about the hens and eggs than I do," Molly said, looking at her daughter who had not put a stitch into her patch while the talk about Bibles had been going on, and whose eyes showed how interested she had been in what was being said.

But now Mary jumped from her low seat, saying, "I'll get what we have, Mrs. Evans."

Presently she came in with a basket containing about a dozen eggs. The farmer's wife put them into her bag, paid for them, then rose to take her leave.

"And remember this, little maid," she said, kindly, when after saying goodbye to Molly she was at the door. "Remember this, my girl; as soon as you know how to read – if by that time you still have no Bible – you may come to the farm when you like, and read and study ours. That is, if you can manage to get so far."

"It's not quite two miles. That's nothing," Mary said, with a glance down at her strong bare feet. "I'd walk further than that for such a pleasure. At least I would, if ever I *did* learn to read."

"Now, never mind, the likes of you wasn't made to sit in the dark always," Mrs. Evans replied in her cheery, comfortable tones. "If the Lord has made you want to read, He'll find the way, be very sure of that. Remember, Mary, when the crowds that went with Jesus were hungry, He didn't send them away empty, though no one knew how they were to be fed. He'll take care you get the bread of life too, however unlikely it seems now. Goodbye, and God bless you, my child," and Mrs. Evans, with a parting nod to Molly Jones, and another to Mary, got into her pony cart which was waiting for her in the road under the care of one of the farm boys.

Mary stood at the door and watched their visitor till she was out of sight. Then her thoughts formed themselves into a prayer something like this: "Dear Lord, You gave bread to the hungry people in the old time, and You taught and blessed even the poorest. Please let me learn, and not grow up in darkness."

Then she shut the door and came and sat down, resolving in her heart that if God heard and answered her prayer, and if she learned to read His Word, she would do what she could, all her life long, to help others as she herself had been helped.

CHAPTER 3

A Surprise

"Please let me learn, and not grow up in darkness," Mary prayed. Two years passed since Mrs. Evans's visit, and still Mary's prayer seemed as far as ever from being answered.

With greater understanding and patience, Mary went about her daily duties. Even though she was young, her mother depended upon her for many things, and Mary had less time for dreaming. Though Cadair Idris was still the spot with which her imagination associated Bible scenes and pictures, she had little time to spare for anything but her everyday duties.

Mary still went with her mother to the midweek meetings at the farm at Llechwedd. From coming into contact with older people, rather than with children of her own age, she would have been called an old-fashioned girl – if she had lived in a place where any difference was known between old fashions and new.

One evening a good friend and neighbor came back from Abergynolwyn, a village two miles away from Llanfihangel. He had been selling the woolen cloth that Molly had been making during the past months.

Mary, whose observant eye was sure to note the slightest sign of excitement in every visitor's face and manner, sprang up and stood before him, regarding his face searchingly.

"What is it?" she asked. "Something pleasant has happened. I know it."

"What a sharp little daughter you have, Molly," the neighbor replied.

"And is it something that concerns me?" Mary asked.

"It is something that concerns you most of all."

"What can it be?" Mary murmured, with a little sigh.

"Yes, what is it?" Mrs. Jones asked, sounding quite impatient herself. "We both want to know."

"Well," the friend replied, "what would you say, Molly, to your daughter here becoming quite a scholar; perhaps knowing how to read and write, and all a deal better than people like us ever did?"

"A school?"

The exclamation came from Mary, who in her excitement now stood breathless with suspense, her hands closely clasped. The friend looked at her a moment without speaking, then he said, "There is a school to be opened at Abergynolwyn, and a master is chosen already. And as you think naught of a two miles' walk, if your mother allows it, Mary, you will be able to go and learn all you can. You are pleased, are you not?"

There was a pause; then Mary's reply came low spoken, but with such deep feeling in its tones. "Pleased? Yes, indeed, for now I shall learn to *read* the Bible."

Then a thought struck her, and a shadow came across her face as she said, "But, mother, perhaps you will not be able to spare me?"

"Spare you? Yes I will, child, though I cannot deny as how it will be difficult for me to do without you as my right hand and help. But for your good, my girl, I would do harder things than that."

"Dear, good mother," Mary cried, putting an arm about Molly's neck and kissing her. "But I don't want you to work too hard and tire yourself. I'll get up an hour or two earlier, and do all I can before I start for school."

Then as the excited girl sat down again to her work, her heart, in its joyfulness, sent up a song of thanksgiving to the Lord who had heard her prayer, and was now opening the way for her to learn, that she might not grow up in darkness.

Presently the visitor spoke again. "I went to see the room where the school is to be held, and who should come in while I was there but Mr. Charles of Bala. I have often heard of him, but I've never seen him, and I was glad to set eyes on him for once."

"What does he look like?" Molly asked.

'Well, I never was a very good one for describing faces, but I should say he was between forty and fifty years old, with a fine big forehead that doesn't look as though it had unfurnished apartments to let behind it, but quite the opposite, as though he had done a sight of thinking and meant to do a great deal more. But his face isn't anything so *very* special till he smiles. Then it's like sunshine, and goes to your heart, and warms you right through. Now I've seen him, and heard him speak, I can understand how he does so much good. I hear he's going about from place to place opening schools for the poor children, who would grow up ignorant otherwise."

"Like me," Mary murmured under her breath.

"And who is the master that is to be set over the school at Abergynolwyn?" Molly asked.

"I heard tell that his name is John Ellis," said the neighbor. "A good man, and right for the work, so they say; and I hope it will prove so."

"And how soon is the school to open?" Mary wanted to know.

"In about three weeks, I believe," the neighbor said.

The following three weeks passed more slowly for Mary Jones than any three *months* she could remember before. The long wait showed itself in impatience. Her home duties at this time were not done so cheerfully or so quickly as usual, for her thoughts were far away, her heart being set on the thing she had longed for so much.

"If *this* is the way it's going to be," her mother said one evening, "I shall wish there had never been a thought of school at Abergynolwyn. Mary, you're so off your head that you go about like someone in a dream. What will it be like when that school begins? I dare not think!"

This longest three weeks that Mary ever spent came to an end at last, and she began to go to school, taking a very important step forward.

What other children called hard work was to Mary only pleasure, and her eagerness was so great that in an incredibly short time she began to read and write.

John Ellis, the schoolmaster, had a quick eye for seeing the character and talents of his pupils. He encouraged Mary in the school, and the girl repaid the master's kindness by working hard and willingly.

Molly Jones could find no fault now with Mary's performance of her home duties. She rose early and did her work before breakfast, and after her return from school in the afternoon she again helped in the home, only keeping for herself time enough to prepare her school lessons for the next day.

At school she was well liked, and never seemed to be regarded with jealousy by her companions, because of the kind way in which she was willing to help others whenever she could.

One morning a small girl was crying when she reached school. On being questioned as to what was the matter, she said that on the way a big dog had snatched at the paper bag in which she was bringing her dinner. The dog had carried it off, and so she would be hungry all day.

Some of the children laughed at the girl for her carelessness, and called her a coward for not running after the dog and getting her dinner back. But Mary whispered something in the girl's ear, dried the wet eyes, and presently the child was smiling and happy again.

When dinner time came, Mary and the dinnerless child sat close together in a corner, and more than half of Mary's provisions found their way to the smaller child.

The other scholars looked on, apparently feeling ashamed that none but Mary Jones had thought of doing so kind and neighborly an action, at the cost of a little self denial. But the lesson was not lost upon them, and often Mary's influence made itself felt in the school for good.

On another occasion Mary was just getting ready to set off on her two mile journey home, when she spied in a corner of the now deserted schoolroom a young boy with a book open before him, and a smeared slate and blunt pencil by his side. Tears were falling over his unfinished task and evidently he was in the last stages of despair. He had dawdled away his time during the school hours, and had not listened when the lesson had been explained. The strict school discipline required that he should stay behind when the rest had gone, and attend to the work that he had left unfinished.

Mary had a headache that day, and was longing to get home. But the sight of that tearful face in the corner banished all thoughts of herself, and as the voices of the other children died away in the distance, she crossed the room and leaned over the boy's shoulder.

"What is it, Robbie? Oh, I see, you've got to do that sum. I mayn't do it for you, you know, because that would be a sort of cheating, but I can tell you how to do it yourself, and I think I can make it plain."

So saying, Mary fetched a little bit of wet rag and washed the slate, and then got an old knife and sharpened the pencil.

"Now," said she, smiling cheerily, "I'll put down the sum as it is in the book." Then she wrote on the slate in clear, if not very elegant figures, the sum in question.

Encouraged now, Robbie gave his mind to his task, and with a little help it was soon done; and Mary with a light heart, which made up for her heavy head, set off home, very glad that what she was herself learning could be a help to others.

Not long after the start of the day school, a Sunday School also was opened. The very first Sunday that children were taught there, Mary appeared as clean and fresh as soap and water could make her. Bright eyes and an eager face showed the keen interest she felt, and her deep wish to learn.

That Sunday evening, after service in the chapel, as Mrs. Evans the farmer's wife was just going to get into her pony cart to drive home, she felt a light touch on her arm.

A young voice she knew, said, "Please, may I speak to you a moment?"

"Surely, my child," the woman replied, turning her smiling friendly face to Mary. "What have you got to say to me?"

"Two years ago, please, you were so kind as to promise that when I'd learned to read you would let me come to the farm and read your Bible."

"I did, I remember it well," Mrs. Evans said. "Well, child, do you now know how to read?"

"Yes, I do," Mary responded. "And I've joined the Sunday School, so there are Bible lessons to prepare. And if you would be so kind as to let me come up to the farm one day in the week – perhaps Saturday, when I have a half-holiday – I could never thank you enough."

"There's no need for thanks, Mary. Come, and welcome. I shall expect you next Saturday, and may the Lord make His Word a great blessing to you. But please remember to take your clogs off at the door!"

Mrs. Evans held Mary's hand one moment, then she got into her cart and the pony started off quickly towards home, as though he knew that old Farmer Evans was laid up with rheumatism, and that his wife wished to get back to him as soon as possible.

CHAPTER 4

Two Miles to a Bible

Mr. Evans' farm was a curious, old-fashioned place. The house was a large rambling building, with many odd ups and downs, and windows in all sorts of unexpected places. And yet there was a homely comfort, not always to be found in far finer and more imposing houses. At the back were the out-buildings – the sheds and cow houses, the poultry pen, the stables and pigsties. Stretching away beyond these again were the home paddock, the drying-ground, and a small enclosed field that went by the name of Hospital Meadow, because it was used for sick animals that needed a rest.

It was the farmer, Mr. Evans, who had spoken so kindly to Mary in the meeting-house at Llechwedd long ago. He was still the same good, honest, industrious, God-fearing man, never forgetting in his work what he owed to the Giver of all, who sends His rain for the watering of the seed, and His sun for the ripening of the harvest.

Nor did he find fault with God if the rain came down upon the hay before it was safely stored, or if an early autumn gale laid his wheat level with the earth from which it sprang, before the sickle could be put into it for harvest. Nor did he complain and grumble even when disease showed itself among the cattle and sheep of which he was justly proud. In short, he was contented with what the Lord sent and with what the Lord allowed.

Mr. and Mrs. Evans had three children. The oldest, a girl, was already grown up and a great comfort and help to her mother. The younger children were boys, who went to a grammar school in a town a little distance away.

Mary remembered to remove her muddy clogs at the door, and was welcomed into the family with love and kindness. But she was shy and timid the first time, for the farmhouse was a much finer place than any home she had previously seen. Yet there was an atmosphere of warmth, and there were signs of plenty, which were unknown in Molly Jones' s poor cottage where there was nothing more than the barest of essentials. But Mary's shyness did not last long.

"Come in, my girl," Mrs. Evans said, drawing Mary into the cozy old-fashioned kitchen that had a kettle singing on the hob. The low-ceilinged room was filled with an enticing fragrance of currant shortcake, baking for an early tea.

"There, get warm, dear," Mrs. Evans continued, "and then you shall go to the parlor and look in the Bible. And have you brought a pencil and some paper to take notes if you want them?"

"Yes, thank you, I brought them with me," Mary replied.

For a few minutes she sat there, basking in the pleasant cheery glow of the firelight. Then she was shown to the parlor where, on the table in the center of the room, was the precious book covered with a clean white cloth. The white cloth was not a sign that the Bible was never used. On the contrary, it was always read at prayers night and morning, for the family loved to study God's Word and seek to understand its teachings.

"There's no need to tell you to be careful of our Bible, and to turn over the pages gently, Mary, I'm sure," Mrs. Evans said. "You would do that anyway, I know. And now, I will leave you and the Bible together. When you've learned your lesson for Sunday School, and read all you want, come back into the kitchen and have some tea before you go."

Then the farmer's wife went away, leaving Mary alone with a Bible for the first time in her life.

It was several minutes before she could bring herself to raise the white cloth. At last folding it neatly, Mary laid it on one side.

Then with trembling hands she opened the book; opened it at the fifth chapter of John, and her eyes caught these words: Chwiliwch yr ysgrythyrau; canys ynddynt hwy yr ydych chwi yn meddwl cael bywyd tragywyddol: a hwynt-hwy yw y rhai sy'n tystiolaethu am danaf fi. ("You study the Scriptures, because you think that in them you will find eternal life. And these very Scriptures speak about me!" John 5:39).

"I will, I will search," she cried, sensing that although the words had first been spoken by Jesus to people who would not accept Him, they were now being spoken directly to her by her Heavenly Father, in His love. "I *will* search *and* learn all I can. Oh, if I had a Bible of my own!"

And this wish, this prayer for the rare and coveted treasure, was a single note in a symphony which, years after, spread in volume, until it rolled in waves of sound over the whole earth. This longing in a young girl's heart was destined to play a part in bringing light and knowledge to millions of souls in the future – a work whose importance is not to be calculated on this side of eternity.

When Mary had finished studying the Bible lesson for Sunday, and had enjoyed a good meal in the cozy kitchen, she said goodbye to her friends and set off home. Her mind was full of the one great longing, out of which a resolution was slowly shaping itself.

And then it was formed at last.

"*I will* have a Bible of my own," she said, surprising herself with the loudness of her voice. "I must have one, if I save up for it for ten years." And by the time this plan had been settled in her mind, Mary reached her home.

Christmas came, and with it some holidays for Mary and the other scholars who attended the school at Abergynolwyn. Mary would have been sorry that lessons stopped, had it not been that during the holidays she determined to carry out her plan for earning something towards buying her Bible.

Without neglecting her home duties, Mary managed to take on work for neighbors. Many were glad to give her a small sum of money. Now it was to mind a baby while the mother was at the washtub. Now to pick up sticks and brushwood in the woods for fuel; or to help to mend and patch the garments of the family for a weary mother, who was thankful to give a small sum for this welcome help.

And every halfpenny, every farthing, was put into a small wooden box. Mary kept the box in a cupboard, on a shelf where she could reach it, and it was a real and heartfelt joy to her when she could bring her day's earnings – the smallest copper coins, perhaps – and drop them in, longing for the time to come when they would have swelled to the required sum – a very large sum unfortunately – for buying a Bible.

Then one day Mrs. Evans, knowing Mary's great wish, and wanting to encourage and help her, made her the present of a fine cockerel and two hens.

"No, no, my dear, don't thank me," she said, when Mary was trying to tell her how grateful she was. "I've done it, first to help you along with that Bible you've set your heart on, and then, too because I love you and like to give you pleasure. So now, my child, when the hens begin to lay, which will be early in the spring, you can sell your eggs, for these will be your very own to do what you like with, and you can put the money to any use you please. And I think I know what you'll do with it," Mrs. Evans added, with a smile.

It happened that the first *silver* coin that Mary had the satisfaction of dropping into her box was earned before she had any eggs to sell. It came in quite a different way from the sums which she had so far received. She was walking home one evening along the road from Tywyn, where she had been sent on an errand. While looking across at the mountains, her foot struck against an object lying in the road. Stooping to pick it up, she found it was a large leather purse. Wondering whose it could be, Mary went on until, within half a mile of home, she met a man walking slowly and evidently searching for something. He looked up as Mary approached, and she recognized him as Farmer Greaves, a relative of Mrs. Evans.

"Ah, good evening, Mary Jones," he said. "I've had such a loss. Coming home from market I dropped my purse, and. . ."

"*I've* just found a purse," Mary said. "Is this it?"

"You've found a purse?" the farmer exclaimed eagerly. "Yes indeed, my dear, that is mine, and I'm very much obliged to you. No, stay a moment," he called after her, for Mary was already trudging off again. "I should like to give you a trifle for your hon. . . I mean, just some trifle by way of thanks."

As he spoke, his finger and thumb closed on a bright shilling, which surely would not have been too much to give to a poor child who had found a heavy purse. But he thought better (or worse) of it, and took out instead a small silver sixpence and handed it to Mary, who took it with very heartfelt thanks, and ran home as quickly as possible to drop her treasure safely into the box – where it was destined to keep its poorer copper brethren company for many a long year.

The Christmas holidays were soon over, and then it was difficult for Mary to keep up with her daily lessons *and* her Sunday School study. The latter meant weekly visits to the farmhouse for reading the Bible. What with these and her home duties, sometimes weeks passed without Mary having time to earn a penny towards the purchase of the Bible.

Sometimes, too, she was rather late in reaching home on the Saturday evenings, and now and again Molly was uneasy about her. For Mary *would* come by short cuts over the hills, along ways which, however safe in the daytime, were rough and unpleasant, if not dangerous, after dark. In these long winter evenings the daylight vanished very early.

It was on one of these occasions that Molly was working at the loom and anxiously waiting for her daughter. Surely Mary had never been as late as this before.

"Mary ought to be home by now," she said aloud, breaking a silence disturbed only by the noise of her busy loom. "It's as dark as dark, and there's no moon tonight. The way's a rugged one if Mary comes the short cut across the fields – and she's not one to choose a long road if she can find a shorter, bless her. She's more than after her time. I hope no harm's come to her," and Molly walked to the window and looked out.

Just then a light step bounded up to the door, the latch was lifted and Mary's young figure entered the cottage, her dark eyes shining, her cheeks flushed, a look of eager animation overspreading the whole of her bright face and seeming to diffuse a radiance round the cottage.

"Well, child, what have you learned today?" Molly asked. "Have you studied your lesson for the Sunday School?"

"Ay, that I have, and a beautiful lesson it was," Mary responded. "It was the lesson, and Mr. Evans together, that kept me so late."

"How so, Mary?" Molly asked, relieved to see her daughter home safely. "I've been so uneasy, fearing lest something had happened to you."

"You needn't have been so, mother," Mary replied, with quiet assurance. "God knew what I was about, and He would not let any harm come to me. Oh, mother, the more I read about Him the more I want to know, and I shall never rest until I have a Bible of my own. But today I've brought home a big bit of the farmer's Bible with me."

"What do you mean, Mary?" her mother asked in dismay. "How could you do such a thing?"

"Only in my head of course," Mary replied, laughing. Then she added, "And in my heart."

"And what is the bit?" her mother asked.

"It's the seventh chapter of Matthew," Mary said. "Our Sunday lesson was from the first verse to the end of the twelfth verse. But it was so easy and so beautiful, that I went on and on, until I'd learned the whole chapter. And just as I had finished, Mr. Evans came in and asked me if I understood it all. And when I said there were some bits that puzzled me, he was so kind and explained them. If you like, I'll repeat the chapter for you."

So Molly pushed away her work, while Mary sat down on a stool. Then beginning at the first verse, she repeated the whole chapter without a single mistake, without a moment's hesitation, and with a tone and emphasis that showed her love and understanding of the words she had learnt.

When Mary repeated the verse, "Ask, and you will receive," Molly saw her daughter's eyes shine and her cheeks aglow, and knew she was thinking of the Bible that she had set her heart on. She had no doubt that Mary was praying for that Bible often enough, even when as her mother she knew nothing about it. And the Lord would give it to Mary some day, of that she was certain. Yes, Molly knew, her Mary would have her Bible.

Again Mary repeated the words of Jesus that she had learned so perfectly: Gofynwch, a rhoddir i chwi; ceisiwch, a chwi a gewch; curwch, ac fe agorir i chwi. Canys pob un sy'n gofyn, sy'n derbyn; ar neb sy'n ceisio, sy'n cael; ac i'r hwn sydd yn curo, yr agorir.

("Ask, and you will receive; seek, and you will find; knock, and the door will be opened to you. For everyone who asks will receive, and anyone who seeks will find, and the door will be opened to him who knocks." Matthew 7:7-8).

CHAPTER 5

The Mysterious Teacher

While Mary was being taught by John Ellis, a twenty-four-year-old man called Lewis Williams, from Pennal, was also learning to read and write. His parents had been too poor to manage any sort of education for him. As he grew up, he was a reckless and wild youth, a trouble to his neighbors, and completely unaware of God and His love. Yet God had a plan for him, too.

These are the words of Saint Paul that changed his life: Eithr y mae Duw yn canmol ei gariad tu ag attom; o blegid a nyni etto yn bechaduriaid, i Grist farw trosom ni. Mwy ynte o lawer, a nyni yn awr wedi ein cyfiawnhâu trwy ei waed ef, y'n hachubir rhag digofaint trwyddo ef.

(But God has shown us how much he loves us – it was while we were still sinners that Christ died for us! By his death we are now put right with God; how much more, then, will we be saved by him from God's anger! Romans 5:8-9).

When he was about eighteen years old, Lewis Williams chanced to be at a prayer meeting where a Mr. Jones of Mathafarn was speaking on this fifth chapter of the Epistle to the Romans.

The word of God came to Lewis Williams in a fresh and striking manner. It was the means of carrying home to his heart the realization of sin. A change was seen in him from that time on. It gradually deepened until none could doubt that he had become a real and committed Christian.

While he was being admitted to membership in a little Methodist church at Cwmllinau, he was asked, "If Jesus Christ asked you to do some work for Him, would you do it?"

His answer gives the key to his success: "Oh yes; *whatever* Jesus required of me I would do *at once.*"

A few years after, when in a place called Trychiad near Llanegryn, he noticed boys in the neighborhood who had no teaching. Filled with a longing to do some special work for his Heavenly Master, he made up his mind to establish a Sunday School, and a weeknight school as well if possible, in order to teach the lads to read their Welsh language.

This would have been nothing remarkable if Lewis Williams had received any sort of education himself. However, as he had never spent a day in school in his life, and could hardly read a word correctly, the thought of teaching others seemed, to say the least, rather a wild idea.

But the old saying has often been proved correct, that where there is a will there is a way, and so it was true in the experience of Lewis Williams.

Through the young man's hard work and courage, his school was opened in a short time, and he began the work by teaching the Welsh alphabet to the lowest class by singing it to the tune of *The March of the Men of Harlech*.

Lewis Williams could hardly restrict his teaching to the lowest class in the school. Yet in teaching the older boys he was coming face to face with an obstacle that might well have seemed too great to anyone with less courage and determination.

The master could not read, or at least he could not read more than a few words, yet he had taken on the work of teaching reading to the lads in his school.

Painfully aware of his lack of knowledge, before commencing his Sunday School work or his evening classes, he used to pay a visit to a woman called Betty Evans who had learned to read well. Under her tuition he prepared the lessons he was going to give that day or the next, so that in reality the master of that flourishing little school was only ahead of his scholars by a few hours.

At other times he would invite a number of boys from the local grammar school to come for reading and discussion. All this was, of course, in the Welsh language.

With quiet tact and careful planning he would arrange that the subject taken should include the lesson which he would shortly have to give.

While the reading and talk went on, he listened with the greatest attention. The discussions as to the meaning or pronunciation of the more difficult words was all that he wanted to find out from the grammar school boys.

But none of these boys had an inkling that the man who invited them, who questioned them so closely, and listened so attentively, was himself a learner, and relied on them for the proper construction of phrases, or for the correct pronunciation of words he would need for his next day's or next week's lessons.

His school days always started with prayer, and as the master had a restless unruly set of lads, he invented a somewhat odd way to get their attention.

Familiar with military drill through once being in the army, he would put the boys through a series of orders, and when they came to "stand at ease," and "attention," he would at once, very briefly and simply, lead them in prayer.While Lewis Williams was hard at work at Llanegryn, seeking to lead people to know Jesus, and train minds to serve Him, it happened that Mr. Charles of Bala arrived at Bryncrug. He was intending to lead a meeting to be held at Abergynolwyn, and spent the night at the house of John Jones, the schoolmaster there.

Mr. Charles asked Mr. Jones if he knew of a suitable person to take charge of one of his recently established schools in the neighborhood.

John Jones replied that he had heard of a young man at Llanegryn, who taught the children both on weeknights and Sundays.

"But," the schoolmaster added, "as I hear that he himself cannot read, I can hardly understand how he is able to teach others."

Thomas Charles

"Impossible," Mr. Charles exclaimed. "How can anyone teach what he does not himself know?"

"Still, they say that he does," John Jones said.

Mr. Charles asked to see this mysterious instructor of youth, who was reported as passing on to others what he did not himself possess The next day, accordingly, summoned by John Jones, the young schoolmaster made his appearance. His old clothes and his rough country manner showed that he was anything but a man of learning.

"Well, my young friend," Mr. Charles said, in the pleasant way that was natural to him, "they tell me you keep a school at Llanegryn yonder, on Sundays and weeknights, to teach children to read. Have you many scholars?"

"Yes, sir, far more than I am able to teach," Lewis Williams replied.

"And do they learn a little by your teaching?" Mr. Charles asked, as kindly as ever, but with a slight hint of disbelief.

"I think some of them learn, sir," the young teacher responded very quietly. A sense of his own feeling of being unequal to the task showed itself painfully both in his voice and manner.

"It is plain that you only speak Welsh. But do you understand *any* English?" questioned Mr. Charles.

"Only a stray word or two, sir, which I picked up when serving in the army."

"Do you read Welsh fluently?"

"No, sir, I can read but little, but I am doing my very best to learn."

"Were you at a school before beginning to teach?" Mr. Charles asked, more and more interested in the young man who stood before him.

"No, sir, I never had a day's schooling in my life."

"And your parents did not teach you to read while you were at home?"

"No, sir, my parents could not read a word for themselves."

Mr. Charles opened his Welsh Bible at the first chapter of the Epistle to the Hebrews, and asked Lewis Williams to read a few verses.

Mr. Williams leant over the Bible as Mr. Charles pointed to these words at the start of the chapter. Duw, wedi iddo lefaru lawer gwaith, a llawer modd, gynt wrth y tadau trwy y prophwydi, yn y dyddiau diweddaf hyn a lefarodd wrthym ni yn ei Fab.

(In the past, God spoke to our ancestors many times and in many ways through the prophets, but in these last days he has spoken to us through his Son. Hebrews 1).

Slowly, hesitatingly, and with several mistakes, the young man stumbled with difficulty through the first verse.

"That will do, my lad," Mr. Charles said. "Just how you are able to teach others to read, passes my understanding. Tell me now, by what plan you instruct the children."

Then the young teacher gave an account of his musical ABC, the lessons given to himself by Betty Evans, the readings and discussions of the grammar school boys, and the scholars playing at "soldiers."

As Lewis Williams proceeded with his confessions (for such they appeared to be to him), Mr. Charles carefully and gently penetrated through the roughness of the teacher to the real force of character of the man. He saw that this follower of Jesus had worked hard to improve his one talent, and work with it in the Master's service, and that he only needed help to become a most valuable servant of Christ. So he recommended Lewis Wiliams to place himself for a time under the tuition of John Jones, to become a more effective school teacher.

During the following three months, Lewis Williams followed the advice of Mr. Charles – and this was all the schooling that he ever had.

Every hour Lewis Williams could spare was devoted to study, in order to fit himself for one of the schoolmasters' places that were under Mr. Charles special control and management. He used to visit neighboring churches, to study the preaching of the ministers there. When he was about twenty-five years of age, he was engaged by Mr. Charles as a paid teacher in one of his schools. He moved to Abergynolwyn a year later, and here, among his pupils, was young Mary Jones.

In later years, Lewis Williams established many new schools and revived others. At length he became a preacher, so great was his ambition in his Master's service, and so anxious was he that all should know the truth and join in the work of the Lord.

And so we return to Mary Jones, who was nearly fifteen years old at the time Lewis Williams became the schoolmaster at Abergynolwyn.

She was as full of life and energy as ever. Nor had her enthusiasm faltered for one moment over her plan for the purchase of a Bible. Through six long years she had hoarded every penny, denying herself the little luxuries which the poverty of her life made so attractive to one so young. She continued her visits to the farmhouse, and the more she studied her Bible lessons for Sunday School, her desire to possess God's Holy Book for herself grew greater rather than less.

What joy it would be, she often thought, if every day she could read and learn by heart passages of Scripture, filling her mind and heart with God's teaching.

"But the time *will* come," she added, "when I shall have my own Bible. Yes, though I have waited so long, the time *will* come." Then on her knees beside her bed she prayed aloud, "Dear Lord, let the time come quickly."

CHAPTER 6

On the Way

"Mother, Mrs. Evans has just paid me for that work I did for her, and it is more than I expected. Now I have enough to buy a Bible. I'm so happy I don't know what to do!"

Mary had just come from the Evans' farmhouse, and as she bounded into Ty'n-y-Ddôl with the joyful news, her mother stopped her and held out both hands.

"Is it really so, Mary? After six years' saving? Well then, God be thanked, who first put the wish into your heart, and then gave you patience to wait and work to get the thing you wanted. Bless you, my child." And Molly laid a hand upon her daughter's head.

"But tell me, mother," Mary said after a little pause, "*where* am I to buy the Bible? There are no Bibles to be had here, *or* at Abergynolwyn."

"I cannot tell you, Mary, but our preacher, William Hugh, will know," Molly replied. "You will do well to go to him tomorrow, and ask how you're to get the book."

Acting on her mother's suggestion, Mary went the next day to Llechwedd to William Hugh, and asked the question so all-important to her. But William Hugh replied that no copy could be obtained locally, and he knew of no place nearer than Bala. Some Welsh Bibles had been printed in Oxford last year, and given to Mr. Charles at a very reasonable price by the Religious Tract Society in London. Then he added that he feared lest all these Bibles had been sold or promised months ago.

This was discouraging news, and Mary went home, cast down but not in despair. There was still, she reflected, a chance that *one* copy of the Bible remained in Mr. Charles' possession – and if so, it would be hers.

The long distance – over twenty-five miles – the unknown road, the far-famed, but to her, strange minister – all this, if it a little frightened her, did not for one moment change her mind. She *would* have the Bible she had saved for all these years.

At first, Molly objected to Mary walking alone all the way to Bala. She would not be able to go with her daughter, for the journey was very difficult.

Then Molly relented. "If it's the Lord's will that you have a Bible," she said, "then He will keep you and lead you safely. It would be wrong of me to try and go against His will."

So Mary had her way, and having received permission for her long journey, she went to a neighbor living near. Telling her of her proposed expedition, Mary asked if she would lend her a bag to carry home the treasure on her shoulder, should she obtain it.

The neighbor, thinking of Mary's many acts of thoughtful kindness towards herself and her children, and glad to be able to show her thanks, put the long bag – called a wallet in Wales – over the girl's shoulder, and bade her goodbye with a hearty "God speed you."

The next morning, a fresh, breezy day in early summer of the year 1800, Mary rose almost as soon as it was light. She washed and dressed with unusual care, for this was to be a day of days – the day for which she had waited for years, and which must, she thought, make her the happiest of girls – *or* bring to her such grief and disappointment as she had never yet known.

Her one pair of Welsh clogs – far too precious a possession to be worn on a twenty-five mile walk – Mary placed in the bag, intending to put them on as soon as she reached the town of Bala.

Early as was the hour, Molly was up to give Mary her breakfast of hot milk and bread, and have prayers, asking specially for God's blessing on Mary's undertaking, and for His protection and care during her journey.

This helped and encouraged Mary, and after kissing her mother she went out into the dawn of that lovely day – a day that she remembered clearly till the last hour of her life.

She set out at a good pace – not too quick, for that would have wearied her before even a quarter of her journey could be done. With an even, steady walk, her bare brown feet treading lightly but firmly along the road, her head held high, her clear eyes glistening, she went – the happiest girl on that day in all the country round. Never before had everything about her looked to Mary as it looked on that memorable morning.

Mary on her way to Bala, with the long wallet over her shoulder

The old mountain of Cadair Idris seemed to gaze down protectingly upon her. The very sun, as it came up on the eastern horizon, appeared to have a smile specially for Mary.

The larks soared from the meadow till their trilling died away in the sky, like a tuneful prayer sent up to God. The rabbits looked out at her from leafy nooks and holes, and even a squirrel, as it ran up a tree, stopped to glance, as much as to say, "Good morning, Mary; have a good journey." The girl's heart was attuned to the loveliness of nature, full of thankfulness for the past, and of hope for the future.

To Mary, Thomas Charles was as yet little more than a name. To those who knew him, he was a mighty man of God.

Thomas Charles of Bala. By many he was called the "Apostolic Charles of Bala" because, like the New Testament apostles, he traveled from place to place, teaching the love and forgiveness of the Lord to people who had never heard the Gospel before. As he went, he started schools. Here adults and children could come and learn about God, and about His Son Jesus who wanted them for His own.

At the age of eighteen Thomas Charles had given himself to Jesus, and his first work for the Lord was in his own home. Here he began family worship, and had an influence as powerful as it was loving and gentle.

The Rev. Thomas Charles became an ordained minister in the Church of England after studying at Carmarthen and Oxford, but owing to the faithful and outspoken style of his preaching, many of his own denomination in those days took offence and would not accept him. So he left the Church of England and joined one of the Welsh Methodist churches. His greatest work, so people said, was the establishment of Day and Sunday Schools in Wales. The organization of these, the selection of paid teachers and visiting the various schools, made Mr. Charles' life a very busy one, but he could see that his hard work was not in vain. Wherever he went he was carrying the Good News, and proving it in his life in the service of Jesus. The darkness that hung over the people lifted, and the true light began to shine.

Such was the man, and such his work up to the time of Mary's journey. Great though this work was, God had even greater plans for him; but he still had some hours left before God would present him with a challenge he would be unable to refuse – for Mary Jones was not yet halfway to Bala.

About the middle of the day Mary stopped to rest, and to eat some of the food which her mother had provided for her. Under a tree in a grassy hollow not far from the road, she half reclined, protected from the sun by the tender green of the spring foliage. Then she began cooling her hot dusty feet in the soft damp grass that spread like a velvet carpet all over the hollow.

Before long Mary spied a little stream, and here she drank, and washed her face and hands and feet, and was refreshed.

Half an hour's quiet rested her thoroughly. Soon she jumped up, slung the bag over her shoulder again and recommenced her journey.

The rest of the way, along a dusty road for the most part and under the warm sun, was now tiring. Mary plodded on, though her feet were blistered and cut with the stones, and her head ached and her limbs were weary.

A kind person in a small cottage gave her a drink of butter-milk as she passed, and a farmer's young daughter, as Mary neared Bala, offered her a share of the supper she was eating as she sat in the porch in the cool of the evening. But Mary could remember nothing more of her journey till she finally got to Bala.

Bala Lake, and Llanycil Church
where Thomas Charles is buried.

On arriving in the town, Mary put on her clogs. Then following the instructions that had been given to her by

William Hugh, she went to the house of David Edwards who was an elderly and much respected Methodist preacher in Bala.

He received her most kindly, questioned her as to why she had traveled far, but ended by telling her that it was now too late in the day to see Mr. Charles.

"But," the old preacher added, seeing his young visitor's disappointment, "you may sleep here tonight, and we will go to Mr. Charles as soon as I see a light in his study window tomorrow morning, so that you may see to your errand in good time, and be able to return home before night."

With grateful thanks Mary accepted the hospitality offered her, and after a simple supper she was shown into the little attic room where she was to sleep.

There, after saying by memory a favorite chapter of the Bible, and speaking with God in prayer, Mary lay down, her mind and body alike resting. Her faith made her sure that her journey would not be in vain, for He who had led her safely this far would surely give her her heart's desire.

Then the curtains of night fell softly around the preacher's humble dwelling. The sleep of those within was sweet, and their safety assured. For, watching over them was the God of the night and the day – the God whom they loved and trusted, and underneath them were the Everlasting Arms.

The center of Bala in the 1880s

CHAPTER 7

Tears

Bala is still a quiet little town, situated near the end of Bala Lake on the north side of a wide, cultivated valley. When Mary Jones walked there for her Bible, it was more quiet and rural still.

Around the town, hills rise to look down upon the large lake. In the town itself, the road is straight and level as it runs past the rugged but often attractive cottages and houses. All was quiet this night, and Mary did not wake until David Edwards, the old preacher, knocked at her door at early dawning.

"Wake up, Mary Jones. Mr. Charles is an early riser, and will soon be at work. The dawn is breaking; get up."

Mary started up, rubbing her eyes. The time had really come, then, and in a few minutes she would know what was to be the result of her long waiting.

Her heart beat quicker as she washed and dressed, but her excitement calmed when she sat down for a minute or two on the side of her bed, and thought of the 23rd Psalm.

Yr Arglwydd yw fy Mugail; ni bydd eisiau arnaf. ("The LORD is my shepherd; I have everything I need." Psalm 23:1).

Mary felt as though she was of a truth being watched over and cared for by a loving Shepherd, and being led by Him. She was soon ready, and with David Edwards she proceeded to Mr. Charles' house without having any breakfast.

Thomas Charles' house in Bala. His wife Sally owned the haberdashery shop, which helped support Thomas Charles' Methodist work financially.

"There's a light in his study," the old preacher said. "Our apostle is at his desk already. There are not many like him, Mary, always at work for the Master. The world would be better if we had more."

Mary did not reply, but she listened intently as David Edwards knocked at the door. There was no answer, only the tread of shoes across the floor. The next moment the door opened, and Mr. Charles himself stood before them.

"Good morning, friend Edwards. And what brings you here so early? Come in, do," said the genial, hearty voice, which so many knew, and had cause to love. Then, as David Edwards entered, Mr. Charles noticed the figure behind him in the doorway.

A rather timid shrinking figure it was now, for Mary's courage was fast ebbing away, and she felt shy and frightened.

A few words of explanation passed between the old preacher and Mr. Charles. Then Mary was invited to enter the study.

"Now, my child," Mr. Charles said, "do not be afraid, but tell me all about yourself, where you live, and what your name is, and what you want."

At this Mary took courage and answered all Mr. Charles' questions; her voice – which at first was low and trembling – strengthening as her confidence returned. She told him all about her home and her mother, and her longing when quite a child for a Bible of her own. Then she told of the long years during which she had saved up her small earnings towards the purchase of a Bible – the sum being now complete.

Then Mr. Charles asked Mary questions as to her Bible knowledge, and was delighted with the girl's replies, which showed how thoroughly she had studied the Book she loved so well.

"But how, my child," he asked in his gentle voice, "did you get to know the Bible as you do, when you do not own one for yourself?"

Mary told him of the visits to the farmhouse, and how, through the kindness of Farmer Evans and his wife, she had been able to study her Sunday School lessons and commit portions of the Bible to memory.

As Mary informed Mr. Charles of all that had taken place, he began to realize how brave, and patient, and earnest and hopeful she had been through all these years of waiting. But when he learned how far Mary had come to obtain possession of the coveted treasure, his bright face became overshadowed.

Turning to David Edwards he said, sadly, "I am indeed grieved that this dear girl should have come all the way from Llanfihangel to buy a Bible, because I am unable to supply her with one. The Welsh Bibles that I received from London last year were all sold out months ago, except for a few copies which I have kept for friends whom I must not disappoint. Unfortunately the Society which has supplied Wales with the Scriptures will not print any more, and where to get Welsh Bibles to satisfy our country's need, I do not know."

Until now, Mary had been looking up into Mr. Charles's face with her great dark eyes full of hope and confidence. But as he spoke these words to David Edwards, she noticed his overclouded face and began to understand the full meaning of his words, and the room seemed to her to darken suddenly.

Dropping into the nearest seat, Mary buried her face in her hands and sobbed. It was all over, then, she said to herself – all of no use – the prayers, the longing, the waiting, the working, the saving for six long years, the weary walk with bare feet, the near prospect of her hopes being fulfilled – all, all in vain.

To a mind so filled with Bible verses as hers, these words of the Psalmist seemed the natural outburst for so great a grief: A anghofiodd Duw drugarhâu? a gauodd efe ei drugareddau mewn soriant? (Has God forgotten to be merciful? Has anger taken the place of his compassion? Psalm 77:9).

All in vain – all of no use. And the young head, lately held so high, drooped lower and lower, and the sunburnt hands, roughened by work and exposure, could not hide the great hot tears that rolled down, chasing each other over cheeks out of which the accustomed rosy tint had fled, and falling unheeded through her fingers. There were a few moments during which only Mary's sobs broke the silence. But those sobs had appealed to Mr. Charles' heart with a strength that he was wholly unable to resist.

With his own voice broken and unsteady, he said, as he rose from his seat and laid a hand on the drooping head of the girl before him, "My dear child, I see you *must* have a Bible, difficult as it is for me to spare you one. It is impossible, yes, simply impossible, to refuse you."

In the sudden burst of feeling that followed these words, Mary could not speak. Instead, she glanced up with such a face of mingled rain and sunshine – such a rainbow smile – such a look of joy and thankfulness in her brimming eyes, that tears filled the eyes of both Mr. Charles and David Edwards.

Mr. Charles turned away for a moment to a bookcase that stood behind him, and opening it, he drew forth a Bible.

Then, laying a hand once more on Mary's head, with the other he placed the Bible in her grasp. Looking down into the earnest glistening eyes upturned to him, he said, "If you, my dear girl, are glad to receive this Bible, truly glad am I to be able to give it to you. Read it carefully, study it, treasure up the sacred words in your memory, and live your life by obeying the Lord's teachings."

And then as Mary was overcome with delight and thankfulness, Mr. Charles turned to the old preacher, and said, huskily, "David Edwards, is not such a sight as this enough to melt the hardest heart? A girl, so poor, so very intelligent, so familiar with the Word of God, compelled to walk all the distance from Llanfihangel to Bala – about fifty miles there and back – to get a Bible. I can never rest until I find some way of supplying our country of Wales which cries out for this Word of God."

Half an hour later Mary Jones was back at David Edwards' house. Here she had her breakfast, before setting off on the long homeward journey.

The day was somewhat cloudy, but Mary did not notice it. Her heart was full of sunshine. The wind blew strongly, but a great calm was in her soul. Her young face was so full of happiness that the folk she met on the way could not help but smile as she skipped happily on, her bare feet seeming hardly to press the ground, and her eyes shining with deep content. The wallet containing her newly-found treasure was no longer slung over her shoulder, but clasped tightly in her arms.

The sun rose and burst through the clouds, glorifying all the landscape. Onward went Mary, her heart, like the lark's song, full of thanksgiving, and her voice breaking out now and again into melody. Sometimes it was the words of some old hymn or of a well-known and much-loved text. They set themselves to music without an effort on her part.

On, still on, Mary went, heeding not the length and weariness of the way. The afternoon came and went. The sun set in the western heavens with a glory that made Mary think of the home prepared above for all God's children. In her mind she could see heaven with its walls of jasper, its gates of pearl, its streets of gold – and its light that needs neither sun nor moon, but streams from the Life-giving Presence of God Himself.

That evening Mary's mother was waiting for supper and for Mary. Had she reached Bala safely? Had she received her Bible? These were just some of the questions that Molly anxiously asked herself, pausing in her work to listen the while for her daughter's return after the tiring and possibly dangerous efforts of her fifty miles' walk.

But Molly Jones was not long kept in suspense. Presently the latch was lifted. Mary entered, weary, footsore, dusty and travel-stained. But she entered with happiness dimpling her cheeks and flashing in her eyes. Molly held out both arms to her daughter, and as she clasped her to her heart, she murmured, "Is all well?"

Mary, from the depths of a satisfied heart, answered with gladness, "All is well."

It so often happens that when a person has wanted something for a long time, possessing it does not bring the happiness expected. Interest in the treasure is quickly lost. It was not so, however, with Mary Jones.

The Bible for which she had toiled, and waited, and prayed and wept, became each day more precious to her. Chapter after chapter she learned by heart, and the study of the Sunday School lessons became her greatest privilege and delight.

Now, if a teacher asked a question that other girls could not answer, Mary was always appealed to, and always seemed ready with a thoughtful and intelligent reply. In committing to memory not only chapters, but whole books of the Bible, Mary was unrivalled both in the Sunday School and in the neighborhood.

Nor was this all. For though to love, and read and learn the Bible are good things, Mary knew it was Jesus who said: O cherwch fi, cedwch fy ngorchymynion. A mi a weddiaf ar y Tad, ac efe a rydd i chwi Ddiddanydd arall, fel yr arhoso gyd â chwi yn dragywyddol. ("If you love me, you will obey my commandments. I will ask the Father, and he will give you another Helper, who will stay with you for ever." John 14:15-16).

Her mother, who had at one time feared that Mary's longing to possess a Bible of her own might lead her to neglect her practical duties, was surprised and delighted to see that, although there was a change indeed in the girl, it was a change for the better. The Holy Spirit was filling her life and teaching her.

The truths that sank into Mary's heart were the precious seed in good ground, which "brings forth fruit a hundredfold." Mary found that there was pleasure in the commonest duties of life, because they were done for the Lord.

Not long after her visit to Bala, Mary had the great pleasure of seeing again the kind friend with whom, in her memory, her Bible would now always be associated.

Thomas Charles, in the course of his visits to the various villages where his schools were established, came to Abergynolwyn to inspect the school there, which was still under the charge of Lewis Williams. Mr. Charles talked with the children personally, to assure himself of their progress.

Memorial to Thomas Charles. It can still be seen in Bala today.

Among the bright young faces upturned to him, his observant eye soon caught sight of one that he had reason to remember with special and with deep interest. The interest deepened still more when he found that from her alone all his most difficult questions received replies.

Thomas Charles did not miss this opportunity of saying a few encouraging words to his young friend, and Mary in her turn treasured the words up, and remembered them through the many years and the various events of her life.

Mary Jones' Bible
It measures 8½ inches (21.5 cm) tall,
6 inches (15 cm) wide, 3¼ inches (8 cm) deep,
and weighs 3 lb 2 oz (1.45 kg)

CHAPTER 8

The Work Begun

There is no doubt that Mary's determined effort to obtain a Bible made a deep impression on the mind and heart of Thomas Charles. Often he thought of that bare-footed girl, her weary journey, and her eagerness to spend her six years' savings on the purchase of a Bible. Then the bitter tears of disappointment, and the tears of joy – all these came back to his recollection again and again. They came blended with the memory of the ignorance and darkness of too many of his countrymen. Thomas Charles knew that a cry was going up all over Wales, from the poor and the rich, for the Word of God. There were times when he thought of nothing else.

In the winter of 1802 Thomas Charles visited London, full of one great thought and plan, though not seeing how it could be carried out. It was while turning the matter over in his mind one morning that the idea occurred to him of a society for the Scriptures – a society set up to publish and distribute God's Holy Word.

Consulting with some of his friends who belonged to the Committee of the Religious Tract Society, he received the warmest encouragement. At their next meeting he spoke about Wales and its lack of Bibles. Although it is not noted in the official records, it is widely believed that Thomas Charles told the story of Mary Jones, to give extra power to his appeal on behalf of his Welsh countrymen.

A great desire took hold of Thomas Charles' hearers to do something towards supplying the great need. The hearts of many were further stirred when one of the secretaries of the Committee, the Reverend Joseph Hughes rose.

In reply to Mr. Charles' appeal for Bibles for Wales, he exclaimed enthusiastically, "Mr. Charles, surely a society might be formed for the purpose; and if for Wales, why not for the world?"

This immediately found an echo in the hearts of many in the audience. So the secretary was instructed to prepare a letter inviting Christians everywhere, of all denominations, to unite in forming a society for spreading God's Word over the whole earth.

Two years passed while plans were made. Then in the month of March 1804, the British and Foreign Bible Society was started, and at its first meeting the sum of £700 was raised, which was a large amount in those days.

Unfortunately, Mr. Charles was unable to be present at this meeting. He was hard at work at home in Wales, but he heard the news with the greatest joy. It was owing to his work and to that of his friends, as well as to the efforts of other Christian workers who deeply felt the great need of the people at this time, that the contributions in Wales alone soon amounted to nearly £1,900. Most of this sum did not come from the rich, but from the poorer people who were now showing their love for the Lord and for their neighbors.

In the Bible Society all denominations helped, brought together by a common cause, and a great wish to serve one common Master. Representatives of the Christian Churches were working together for the good and enlightenment of the world, by bringing people to know and love Jesus.

Great was the joy and thankfulness of this hard-working minister of Christ, when he learnt that the first work of the Committee of the Bible Society would be to bring out an edition of the Welsh New Testament for use in Welsh Sunday Schools. And his delight was greater still when the first consignment of these New Testaments reached Bala in 1806, and a Welsh edition of the whole Bible exactly a year later.

"Beibl i bawb o bobl y byd," ("A Bible for all the people in the world,") became a popular saying amongst Welsh Christians.

On leaving school Mary Jones worked as a weaver, while still living with her mother. In the early 1800s they moved to Cwrt, on the edge of Abergynolwyn. Mary's precious Bible was as dear to her as ever. She was intensely interested in the founding of the Bible Society, and in the news of the first edition of the new Welsh Bibles arriving at Bala.

In addition to her weaving, and the household help she gave her mother who was now neither well nor strong, Mary had become good at dressmaking. This stood her in good stead when she wished to earn a little extra money.

All who could afford it came to her to cut out and make their dresses, and though Mary never wasted a moment, she sometimes found it quite difficult to do during the day all that she had planned.

Occasionally Mr. Charles would visit Abergynolwyn. At such times he and Mary Jones met again, and she would learn from him how the Society in London was going on – that great London that was a strange, distant, untried world to her. She had only vague ideas of its size and its distance from the quiet, secluded place where she lived.

All the while, up in London, the great tree of life went on growing and spreading. And the girl who had played a part in this – Mary Jones – remained in Wales, almost unseen. God was showing that He had need of the high and the lowly, the great and the small.

CHAPTER 9

The Work Goes On

When next we visit this part of Wales, Mary is no longer Mary Jones. A great change has come over her surroundings. Her school work and her old home life with her mother are things of the past.

She has married a weaver, Thomas Jones, the son of Lewis Jones. Thomas was called by his father's name of Lewis, as was the custom then, and so was known as Thomas Lewis. Thomas and Mary are living at the village of Bryncrug, between Tywyn to the west, and Llanfi-hangel and Abergynolwyn to the east.

This has been a sad time for Mary, as well as a happy one. Molly Jones, who had brought her up to know and love the Lord and Savior, has died. But Mary knew that in heaven her mother and father were happy, and for them all suffering and unhappiness was in the past.

So here at Bryncrug, with a husband and children of her own, with new duties and fresh cares, Mary's love for her Bible was still growing. Sadly, as with so many poor families at that time, three of their children – Mary, Benny and a second Mary – died while very young, their son Jacob died aged fifteen, Lewis died aged eighteen, and only John lived on. He eventually emigrated to America, and some people think he took one of Thomas Charles' Bibles with him.

Bryncrug

Things changed – friends, home influences, claims, interests – but God's Word remained to Mary unaltered, except that every day it grew more into her heart and became more one with her life. From careful study, and prayer for God's Spirit to open her eyes to deeper meanings, Mary discovered truths in the Bible that had been unnoticed by her before.

Mary's life had been a busy one during the years spent at Llanfihangel and Cwrt, but doubly so was her life here at Bryncrug. Yet for all her hard work, Mary had a way of making every duty, however humble and simple, a service for Jesus. So, by her Christian life she influenced the people she met from day to day.

If a neighbor's child wished to have a Sunday School lesson explained, she invariably came to Mary, who could always spare a few minutes to give the same instruction that had been so precious to her in her childhood days. And Mary's good knowledge of the Bible gave her a very clear way of explaining its truths. She was now a wise counselor and teacher.

If, again, a friend wanted a hint or two in making a new dress, or advice over the management of her beehives, Mary was always the authority appealed to. She was known as the most capable, as well as the kindest of neighbors, and ever ready to lend a helping hand, or speak a helpful word.

So, in Bryncrug, Mary was winning the love and confidence of her neighbors, and showing in her life and character the love of the Savior whose faithful servant she tried to be. Mary was certainly an authority on bees, as her success with her own beehives proved. That success was simply remarkable, both in the large number of hives, and their profitable results.

The power and influence that Mary seemed to exercise over people appeared to extend even to her bees. Whenever she went near the hives, her reception by her winged subjects was nothing less than royal.

The air would be thick with buzzing swarms, and presently they would alight upon her by hundreds, covering her from head to foot, walking over her but never attempting to sting, or showing any feeling but one of absolute friendliness. She would even catch a handful of them, but softly, so as not to hurt them. They never misunderstood her, or gave her the slightest injury. In short, there seemed to be some close understanding between Mary and her bees, and they were the means of earning money to go towards the support of God's work in the world.

The money brought by the sale of the honey was used for the family and household expenses, but the money from the sale of the wax was divided among the Christian societies which, poor as the family was, Mary wanted to help.

Among these, foremost in her estimation stood the British and Foreign Bible Society. In later years this Society was to join with other Bible Societies, to form the large, worldwide United Bible Societies we know today. Mary had played a part in the founding of the British and Foreign Bible Society, maybe only a small part, but she was never happier than when she could spare what for her was a large sum, to help in sending the Word of God – so precious to her own heart – over the world.

Mary was also very interested in the Calvinistic Methodist Missionary Society – a Society founded by the denomination to which she had, for so many years, belonged. Secretly she gave up many things, so there would be money to spare for the work of the Gospel.

On one occasion, when a collection was made at Bryncrug for the China Million Testament Fund in 1854, a gold coin – a half sovereign – was found in the collection plate. It was concealed between two copper half-pence, and thus hidden until the money came to be counted.

This was Mary's gift, the gift of a loving and generous heart touched both by God's love, and by the spiritual needs of people throughout the world.

Mary was sitting at her cottage door one day when a neighbor, Betsy Davies, came up and asked if she could sit with her. "I have a dress I'm altering for my eldest girl," she explained, "and I don't see how to finish it. I thought maybe you'd be good enough to show me."

Betsy Davies laid the dress over Mary's knee, and Mary's eyes, quick and intelligent as ever, saw in a moment or two what was needed.

"That's not a difficult job," she said pleasantly. "Just unpick that seam, Betsy, and I'll pin it for you as it ought to be. Then if you let down the tuck in the skirt, you'll have it long enough; and as for that torn part, I think I have some thread about the right color to darn it up. I will show you how I darn my children's clothes. Yours can be mended in the same way, and you will see it will hardly show at all."

When the two women had settled down to their work, Betsy said, "I wish you'd tell me, Mary, how you manage to get on as you do. You can't be rich people. You and your husband are weavers – like most of us here. Yet you never get into debt, and you always seem to have enough for yourselves. And what's more amazing still, you have enough to give something away too. I must say I can't understand it."

"I don't think there's anything very hard to understand," Mary said, smiling. "If by being careful, and giving some things up, we can help in God's work, it is surely the greatest joy we can have."

"Yes, that's all very well," Betsy replied, "but I never have anything to give. Yet I haven't as many children as you, and so my family and housekeeping doesn't cost so much."

"It's like this, Betsy," Mary explained. "We ask ourselves 'What can I do without?' And each of us in the family is willing to give up some little luxury, and so we save the money. We put it into a box that we call the treasury. Then, whenever we add anything to what we keep there, we think of the widow who dropped her two mites into the treasury of the temple, and how Jesus said such loving words about her."

"But what *sort* of things can you give up?" Betsy asked. "We poor folk, it seems to me, don't have any more than just the necessities of life. We can't give up eating, or go without clothes to our backs."

"That's true," Mary agreed, "but I think if you consider a bit, you'll see there are some things which are not really essential, though they may be pleasant. Now for instance, Thomas had always been used to a pipe and a bit of tobacco in an evening after his work was done. But when we were all wondering what we could give up for our Lord's sake, he said, 'I'll give up my smoke in the evenings.' And I tell you, Betsy, the tears came into my eyes when I heard that, knowing that my husband's words meant a real sacrifice. Then our eldest son, Lewis, wishing to follow his father's example, cried out, 'And I still have the Christmas money I was given last winter, and I'll give that.'"

"And you yourself?" Betsy asked, with interest.

"I? Oh, I have the wax that my bees make. The money I get by selling the wax goes into the treasury, as well as any other small sum I do not *really* need. And I must say, Betsy, we have never really suffered for the want of anything that we have given to God. He repays us with such happiness and content as He alone can give."

"That I can well believe," Betsy agreed, "for I never hear you grumble, or see you look cross or discontented like so many of the neighbors – as I do myself only too often. Well, Mary," she continued, "I mean to try your plan, though it will come very hard at first, as I'm not used to that sort of saving."

"I think I got used to it when I was just a girl, putting away my money towards buying a Bible," Mary answered.

"For six years I put aside all I had, and since then it has come natural."

"You did get your Bible, then?"

"Yes, indeed." Rising from her seat Mary took the much prized volume from the table in the cottage, and put it into her friend's hands. "This is the very one."

Betsy looked at it, inside and out, then handed it back, saying, "I really believe, Mary, that this Bible is one of the reasons why you are so different from all the rest of us. You've read, and studied and learnt so much of it, that your thoughts and words and life are full of it."

Mary turned her bright dark eyes, now full of happy tears towards her companion. "Oh, Betsy dear, if there is a little, even a little truth in what you say of me, I thank God. Even now I am surprised that He allows me, poor and weak though I am, to show to others the truths of His Word. And, Betsy, He *wants* me to do it."

"But, Mary, you're a special person," Betsy said. "That's why He uses you."

Can you imagine Mary shaking her head and saying: "No, Betsy, you're wrong. God needs us all. Perhaps we will never understand just how much we are needed. It was Jesus, the Son of God, who said: Onid ydych chwi yn dywedyd, Y mae etto bedwar mis, ac yna y daw'r cynhauaf? Wele, yr ydwyf fi yn dywedyd wrthych, Dyrchefwch eich llygaid, ac edrychwch ar y meusydd; canys gwynion ydynt eisoes i'r cynhauaf. – You have a saying, 'Four more months and then the harvest.' But I tell you, take a good look at the fields; the crops are now ripe and ready to be harvested!" (John 4:35)

I can see Mary pointing across the small town, over the mountains, sweeping her arms to include the whole world. "And who is going to reap the harvest for God if you and I don't do it, Betsy? Who *will* be a laborer for the Lord?"

MARY JONES' COTTAGE

How the cottage in Llanfihangel probably looked
when Mary Jones was born there in 1784.

Mary Jones' cottage in the 1880s, from
Mary Ropes' book dated 1890.

All that is left of Mary Jones' cottage today,
with the memorial inside.

WHERE TO FIND THINGS

Mary Jones' cottage is beyond Saint Michael's Church in
Llanfihangel-y-Pennant, (Llanfihangel means the Church of
Saint Michael), by the small bridge over the river. It is clearly
marked. There is a permanent exhibition about Mary Jones in
Saint Michael's Church. In the churchyard is the grave of
Mary's parents, just beyond the main doorway, marked by a
very small slate memorial stone. Opposite the church is a
footpath leading up into the woods, a very short walk to the
dilapidated meeting-house at Llechwedd. There are several
chapels in Abergynolwyn, but the original Methodist chapel
used by Mary and her mother is down by the river, and has now
been converted into housing. Mary and her husband are buried
at the Methodist Chapel at Bryncrug. The grave is large, up the
slope, and very noticeable.

SOME NOTES

It would be a mistake to think that Mary Jones was the reason the Bible Society was founded. She was just one of many people who walked long distances, anxious to get a Bible. But Mary's story was an important link in a chain that led to the founding of the British and Foreign Bible Society, though certainly not the only link. Nor, of course, was Thomas Charles the only person involved in the founding of the Society. So what marks Mary out as a special person? It is this. Over the past two hundred years her story has been told countless times, inspiring young people to give themselves to God's work – when they realize that God needs and uses ordinary people.

It is likely that Mary saved up more than was needed for one of the heavily subsidized Bibles from London, and when she got to Bala in 1800 she discovered she had enough for two, possibly even three copies. Mary definitely gave one Bible from this 1799 printing to her aunt. Some accounts say that Thomas Charles gave Mary the extra one without charge, or maybe even two extra. Although it's possible Mary brought back more than one Bible from Bala, this is unlikely. Not only were these Welsh Bibles in very short supply, they were heavy. Probably Thomas Charles brought the extra one (possibly two) Bibles from a new delivery when he was next in the Llanfihangel area. The Bible Mary gave to her aunt is in the National Library of Wales in Aberystwyth. Her own Bible is safely in the Cambridge University Library, showing considerable signs of wear and tear from heavy use.